# READERS

## Level 2

## Level 3

# A Note to Parents

DK READERS is a compelling program for beginning readers, designed in conjunction with leading literacy experts, including Dr. Linda Gambrell, Distinguished Professor of Education at Clemson University. Dr. Gambrell has served as President of the National Reading Conference, the College Reading Association, and the International Reading Association.

Beautiful illustrations and superb full-color photographs combine with engaging, easy-to-read stories to offer a fresh approach to each subject in the series. Each DK READER is guaranteed to capture a child's interest while developing his or her reading skills, general knowledge, and love of reading.

The five levels of DK READERS are aimed at different reading abilities, enabling you to choose the books that are exactly right for your child:

**Pre-level 1:** Learning to read
**Level 1:** Beginning to read
**Level 2:** Beginning to read alone
**Level 3:** Reading alone
**Level 4:** Proficient readers

The "normal" age at which a child begins to read can be anywhere from three to eight years old. Adult participation through the lower levels is very helpful for providing encouragement, discussing storylines, and sounding out unfamiliar words.

No matter which level you select, you can be sure that you are helping your child learn to read, then read to learn!

LONDON, NEW YORK, MUNICH,
MELBOURNE, and DELHI

## For DK/BradyGames

**Title Manager** Tim Fitzpatrick
**Cover Designer** Tim Amrhein
**Production Designer** Tracy Wehmeyer
**Global Strategy Guide Publisher** Mike Degler
**Editor-In-Chief** H. Leigh Davis
**Licensing Manager** Christian Sumner
**Marketing Manager** Katie Hemlock
**Digital Publishing Manager** Tim Cox
**Operations Manager** Stacey Beheler

## For DK Publishing

**Publishing Director** Beth Sutinis
**Licensing Editor** Nancy Ellwood
**Reading Consultant** Linda B. Gambrell, Ph.D.

## For WWE

**Global Publishing Manager** Steve Pantaleo
**Photo Department** Frank Vitucci,
Josh Tottenham, Jamie Nelson, Mike Moran,
JD Sestito, Melissa Halladay, Lea Girard
**Legal** Lauren Dienes-Middlen

DK/BradyGAMES
800 East 96th St., 3rd floor
Indianapolis, IN 46240

14 15 16 10 9 8 7 6 5 4 3 2 1

A catalog record for this book is available
from the Library of Congress.

ISBN: 978-1-4654-2088-6 (Paperback)
ISBN: 978-1-4654-2106-7 (Hardback)

Printed and bound by Lake Book

The publisher would like to thank the following for their kind
permission to reproduce their photographs:
All photos courtesy WWE Entertainment, Inc.

All other images © Darling Kindersley
For further information see: www.dkimages.com

Discover more at
# www.dk.com

# DK READERS

BEGINNING TO READ ALONE

2

# John Cena ®
## SECOND EDITION
### Written by Kevin Sullivan

John Cena became a WWE fan when he was a young boy. He sat in front of his television every Saturday morning as Hulk Hogan, Andre the Giant, Ultimate Warrior, and the rest of WWE's Superstars competed in the ring. Their athleticism and colorful personalities caught the young Cena's imagination. He was so captivated that he even created cardboard titles and wore them around the house, pretending to be like the champions he watched on television.

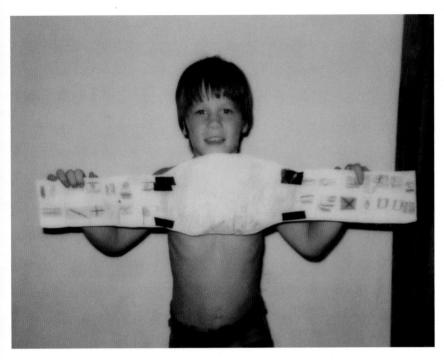

Cena also loved hip-hop music and fashion. He liked to make up his own songs, but they weren't very popular in his hometown of West Newbury, Massachusetts. The other kids in his town listened to hard rock music. They teased Cena for being different.

However, Cena didn't pay attention to the kids that teased him. He just kept doing what made him happy.

The teasing finally stopped when Cena started bodybuilding at the age of 15.

The more Cena exercised, the stronger he became. As Cena's muscles got bigger, the other kids stopped picking on him.

After high school, Cena went to Springfield College. He was the captain of the football team and earned a degree in exercise physiology.

**John Cena Stats**

**Height:** 6'1"

**Weight:** 251 lbs.

**From:** West Newbury, Massachusetts

**Signature Moves:** Attitude Adjustment, STF

Cena began working at a gym in California after college. While there, he met another bodybuilder who urged him to try to become a WWE Superstar.

Cena liked the idea, but he knew it would be hard work. Hoping to learn the proper way to compete, he enrolled in the Ultimate Pro Wrestling school in 2000.

## John Cena Facts

- Nobody has held the WWE Championship more times than John Cena.
- John Cena has won Tag Team Championships with Shawn Michaels, Batista, David Otunga, and The Miz.
- John Cena appeared on *Saturday Night Live* in 2009.
- John Cena has more than 5.8 million Twitter followers and 17 million Facebook Likes.

Cena learned very quickly. Within weeks, his training paid off when he won the UPW Heavyweight Championship in April. Soon, WWE officials learned about the young competitor and signed him to a contract. They sent him to Ohio Valley Wrestling to complete his training and learn how to become a WWE Superstar.

Cena became an official WWE
   Superstar in June 2002. His first
   match was against Kurt Angle.
   Cena lost the match, but
     showed great determination
     and willpower. It was clear
     that Cena was going to be
 a big star.

The young Cena defeated many top stars over the next few months, including Chris Jericho. He also started to show some of the traits he had while growing up.

Just like he did when he was a boy, Cena began wearing hip-hop clothes and rapping before matches. This time, though, nobody made fun of him. Cena was respected by everybody around him because of his hard work and determination.

By 2004, Cena had become one of WWE's top Superstars. Many fans saw January's *Royal Rumble* as his big chance to earn a WWE Championship Match at *WrestleMania*.

However, Cena's dreams of winning the Rumble Match were crushed when he was thrown over the top rope by Big Show.

Cena gained revenge from Big Show when he defeated the giant.

This won him the United States Championship at *WrestleMania XX*. It was Cena's first of many WWE title wins.

Cena held the U.S. Championship three different times in 2004. During this time, he replaced the traditional title with a new one that featured a spinning American flag in the center.

In 2005, Cena earned a WWE
Championship Match against JBL
at *WrestleMania 21*. It was the
biggest match of Cena's career up
to that point. Fans from all over
the world watched to see if he
really was good enough to beat the
reigning champ.

Lesser Superstars would've folded under the pressure of competing on WWE's biggest stage. John Cena didn't. Instead, he proved he was WWE's best when he pinned JBL after delivering an Attitude Adjustment.

Just like his heroes before him, John Cena was WWE Champion. Shortly after the win, Cena once again revealed his own version of the title. This one featured a spinning WWE logo in the center.

Winning the title at *WrestleMania* meant that Cena was the best Superstar in WWE. He was also quickly becoming a huge star outside of WWE. Shortly after becoming champ, Cena released his own rap album called *You Can't See Me.*

The album was a big success. It even debuted at number 15 on the *Billboard* charts.

That's not all. Cena also completed the filming of his first starring role in a major motion picture, *The Marine.* With so much going on in and out of the ring, Cena was becoming one of the biggest stars in WWE history.

## John Cena Movies

- *The Marine*
- *12 Rounds*
- *Legendary*
- *Fred: The Movie*
- *The Reunion*
- *Fred 2: Night of the Living Fred*
- *Fred 3: Camp Fred*
- *Scooby-Doo! WrestleMania Mystery*

*The Marine*

Cena's title reign was cut short in January 2006. Edge defeated him for the WWE Championship at *New Year's Revolution*.

Cena didn't let the loss get him down. Instead, he focused all his attention on winning back the gold. Just three short weeks after the loss, he beat Edge to reclaim the title.

With the gold back around his waist, Cena defeated some of WWE's biggest names, including Big Show and Randy Orton. He even used his STF submission to beat Triple H at *WrestleMania 22*.

The following year at *WrestleMania* 23, he used the same move to beat Triple H's longtime friend Shawn Michaels.

Cena held the WWE Title for more than one year before Randy Orton injured the champ's right pectoral muscle in October 2007. The injury was so severe that Cena needed immediate surgery. He was forced to give up the WWE Championship.

Doctors told Cena he could be out of action for up to one full year. However, after less than four months of grueling rehab, he made a surprise return at the 2008 *Royal Rumble*. He last eliminated Triple H to win the Rumble Match. It was the first of two *Royal Rumble* victories for Cena.

2008
Royal
Rumble

Heading into *Survivor Series* 2008, Cena had already won nearly every major championship there was to win.

However, one major title had eluded him his entire career: The World Heavyweight Championship. That night, Cena defeated Chris Jericho in the main event. He claimed his first of three World Heavyweight Championship reigns.

Cena was the target of a vicious attack by The Nexus in June 2010. Led by Wade Barrett, the renegade group spent the rest of the year trying to prove their superiority over Cena. At one point, Barrett even beat Cena. Because of the loss, Cena was forced to temporarily join The Nexus.

Cena eventually got his revenge on his rivals. He defeated Barrett in a Chairs Match at *WWE TLC* in December 2010. The following month, Cena eliminated many Nexus members from the *Royal Rumble* match. This marked the end of their lengthy rivalry.

Hoping to regain the WWE Championship, Cena challenged The Miz at *WrestleMania XXVII*. Unfortunately, The Rock interfered in the match and landed a Rock Bottom on Cena. From there, The Miz slid in and pinned Cena for the win.

The next night on *Raw*, Cena challenged The Rock to a match. The Rock quickly accepted, and the contest was set for *WrestleMania XXVIII*. This was the very first time that the biggest show of the year's main event was set one full year ahead of time.

Two of the biggest names in WWE history finally collided when Cena and The Rock squared off at

*WrestleMania XXVIII*. It was one of the biggest matches of all time. When the dust from the dream match cleared, The Rock stood tall as the winner. However, Cena wasn't done with The Rock yet.

After winning the 2013 *Royal Rumble*, Cena chose to battle The Rock once again at *WrestleMania*. This time, the stakes were even higher. The Rock's WWE Championship was on the line. In the end, Cena gained revenge from his previous year's loss. He pinned Rock to win the WWE Championship.

John Cena has been WWE's top star for nearly a decade. Every time he  enters an arena, he knows that "Hustle, Loyalty, and Respect" can help him be a champion inside and outside the ring. No matter how down he feels, he's reminded to "Never Give Up." Because of this hard work and dedication, John Cena has become one of the all-time greatest WWE Superstars.